Dia's Story Cloth

written by **DIA CHA**

stitched by

CHUE and **NHIA THAO CHA**

compendium by **JOYCE HEROLD,**
Curator of Ethnology, Denver Museum of Natural History

LEE & LOW BOOKS, Inc., 95 Madison Avenue, New York, NY 10016

Printed in Hong Kong by South China Printing Co. (1988) Ltd.

Published in cooperation with the Denver Museum of Natural History:
Project Manager: Betsy Armstrong, DMNH
Photography by Rick Wicker, DMNH

Book design by Christy Hale
Book production by The Kids at Our House

The text is set in Garamond 3
The story cloth and all objects pictured in the compendium are from
the Hmong Collection, Laos and Thailand, Denver Museum of Natural History.
The actual story cloth measures 66 inches high and 103 inches wide.

A portion of the proceeds from this book will benefit
The Hmong Women's Education Association of Colorado, Denver, CO.

10   9   8   7   6   5   4   3   2   1
First Edition

Library of Congress Cataloging-in-Publication Data
Cha, Dia
Dia's story cloth/written by Dia Cha; stitched by Chue and Nhia Thao Cha.—1st ed.
p.   cm.
Summary: The story cloth made for the author by her aunt and uncle
chronicles the life of the Hmong people in their native Laos
and their eventual emigration to the United States.
ISBN 1-880000-63-6 (paperback)
1. Hmong (Asian people)—Juvenile literature. 2. Hmong Americans—Juvenile literature.
3. Embroidery, Hmong—Themes, motives—Juvenile literature.
[1. Hmong (Asian people) 2. Hmong Americans. 3. Embroidery, Hmong.]
I. Cha, Chue, ill. II. Cha, Nhia Thao, ill. III. Title.
DS509.5.H66D53   1996
973'.0495—dc20   95-41465
                                                            CIP   AC

This is my story

THIS STORY CLOTH SHOWS THE JOURNEY OF MY PEOPLE. We are called Hmong, which means "free people." Our journey begins long ago in China, and continues to Laos and then the refugee camps in Thailand. For over 125,000 Hmong people, the journey ends in the United States.

My Aunt Chue and Uncle Nhia Thao Cha sent this story cloth to me and my mother from the Chiang Kham refugee camp in Thailand. I will never forget the day the story cloth arrived in the mail five years ago. When I looked at the pictures in the cloth, I remembered how my own family came to the United States in 1979, when I was 15 years old.

Everything in a Hmong story cloth is hand-embroidered. Only the women used to do needlework, but since so many of our people have been detained in refugee camps, men, like my Uncle Nhia, help make story cloths to pass the time and earn money. It takes many months to complete a story cloth. No patterns are used; no measurements are made. The needlework is done by eye, and comes out perfectly every time.

Here in the United States, stories are told in a different form, through illustrations in a book. But Hmong people living here today continue the tradition of needlework. The stitches in a Hmong story cloth make pictures of life. This story cloth will tell you about our life.

Along time ago, my ancestors lived in China. The ancient Chinese government wanted to change the way the Hmong lived. But my people would not give up their culture, and fled on foot across the river and through jungles to southeast Asia. Some went to Burma; some went to Thailand. Like many Hmong, my ancestors migrated to Laos.

When they arrived in Laos, the Hmong settled in the tropical highlands where no one had lived before. They had to clear forests to build their villages and plant their crops. They grew corn and rice.

The daily life in the Hmong villages included working in the fields from morning to night. Both men and women tended the crops. Everything from tools to food was carried in different kinds of baskets on their backs.

In Laos, the Hmong were able to farm as they wished and lived in peace for many years.

When I was a child, in the 1960s, my family lived in a wood and bamboo house with a thatched roof made of palm leaves. Every morning I helped my mother and sisters pound rice. After breakfast, my family walked for almost two hours to our mountainside fields, where we worked all day. Every evening we walked back home. At harvest time we each carried a backpack basket filled with rice or corn.

But as I was growing up, the peaceful life of my village was disappearing.

Laos was caught in warfare. My country was divided in two: On one side, many Hmong men joined the loyalist army, which was supported by the American government. On the other side was the communist regime, which also recruited many Hmong men.

My father left to fight with the loyalist troops. My family began to move from village to village to escape the communist soldiers.

Communist soldiers came to the Hmong villages and captured the men. They tied the Hmong's hands behind their backs and took them away. The Hmong men kneeled down and begged for their lives, but the soldiers didn't listen. The Hmong women couldn't do anything to help. They cried and cried because they knew they might never see their husbands and sons again.

My father was sent to fight in Xieng Khuang province. He never came back. We don't know whether he was killed or captured.

Airplanes dropped bombs on the Hmong villages. Many houses were destroyed by flames. Women and children fled into the jungle and lived in huts made from banana leaves. I remember having to get up in the middle of the night, feeling so afraid because we had to flee our hiding place. Sometimes we hid in the forest, or in caves until the communist soldiers left.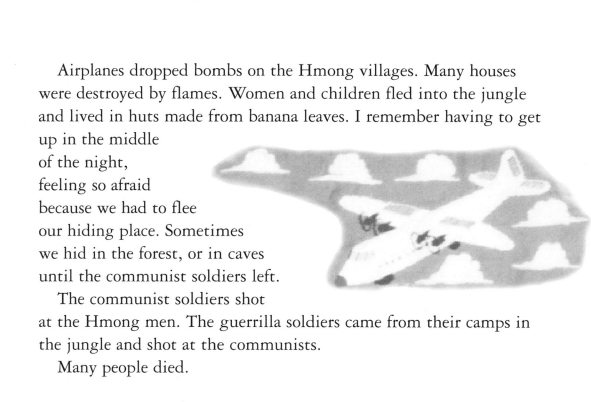

The communist soldiers shot at the Hmong men. The guerrilla soldiers came from their camps in the jungle and shot at the communists.

Many people died.

In 1975 the Americans pulled out of Laos and the communist regime took over. My mother was determined to get us out of Laos. I was 10 years old when we fled.

Escaping meant we had to cross the Mekong River. But the river was dangerous. People who didn't have boats had to cross by swimming or using inner tubes and bamboo poles to stay afloat. Many people died trying to cross this river.

Like other escaping Hmong, we lived in a refugee camp when we arrived in Thailand. We lived in barracks. Some families planted small gardens. All the Hmong were very homesick.

Earlier in Laos, my mother had destroyed all the documents we had relating to my father and the war. So we didn't have anything to prove my father was actually fighting on the side of the Americans. But when we got to the camp, one of my father's friends gave us a photo of my father taken at the front lines.

The U.S. government sent staff to interview the Hmong refugees to determine who would be able to emigrate to America. When the American lady came to interview us, the photo of my father was our proof that we were qualified as political refugees. In 1979, after four and a half years in the camp, we left Thailand for America.

As the buses left the camp, we said goodbye to all the people we knew. In some families there were members who had to stay behind in Thailand, while their relatives were allowed to go to America. Many people cried.

When my people first arrived in America, most didn't speak or write English. Many families had sponsors, who picked us up at the airport.

Everything about life in America was different for the Hmong.

I was 15 years old when I came to this country. I'd never been to school, so I had to start everything from scratch. They wanted to put me in high school, but I didn't know anything. Then they wanted to put me in an adult school, but the teachers said I was too young.

Finally, I started high school. Thirteen years later, I received my master's degree from Northern Arizona University. I went back to Laos as an anthropologist in 1992 to work with Hmong and Lao women in the refugee camps in Thailand.

This story cloth reminds me of the history of my family and of my people. Some of the memories it brings are good, and some are bad. But it is important for me to remember everything the Hmong have been through.

Hmong women in America continue to stitch new story cloths. We all have vivid memories about our lives and culture and history. The story cloth is a bridge to all the generations before us. When I show the story cloth to my niece and nephew, who were both born here in the United States, I point to different pictures and tell them that this is what it was like.

Hmong means Free People

A nation of immigrants—in fact, *many* nations of immigrants—Americans tell numerous tales of how we got here. Some of the most recent and most extraordinary odysseys can be told by America's refugee populations. Most from Southeast Asia have fled a generation of war in search of freedom. Offered havens by American allies, they have come to the United States with rich cultural traditions upon which to build new lives. They are our neighbors.

One such tale is told in this book. Dia Cha and her family's escape to the United States is a story that is shared by many Hmong Americans. The name "Hmong" (pronounced "Mong") translates as "Free People."

Through a newly invented folk art form—the embroidered story cloth—Hmong artists and needleworkers remember how they *lived* the picture stories sewn on cloth. Hmong Americans describe how their pursuit of freedom fueled escape to North America and Europe. It is an odyssey that began in centuries past but culminated during the last 20 years.

Who are these people, the Hmong Americans? Where and how have they created their unique needlework designs? In what context can we place this particular cloth and Dia's story?

In 1976, under the auspices of world relief organizations, the first Hmong refugee families came from Laos and Thailand to the United States, settling in California, Oregon, Montana, Minnesota, Wisconsin, Iowa, and Colorado, with other Southeast Asian immigrants, such as the more numerous Vietnamese. The Hmong had been known throughout Southeast Asia for their exquisite needlework. Soon after arriving in the United States, their "flower cloth," or *pa'ndau* (pronounced "pan-**dow**") began to

White Hmong back-carrying baskets, in child and adult sizes.

appear at local community fairs. This striking needlework soon came to distinguish the approximately 125,000 Hmong Americans.

According to their history, forebears of the Hmong lived on the Central Plain of China as early as 2300 B.C. Later, they were known as the Miao to the Chinese, who pushed them to the southern borderlands of China. In the mid-19th century, the Hmong began moving further southward and settled the highland fringes of what was then known as Indochina and Burma. The people founded villages of wood, bamboo, and palm leaf thatch houses on mountains throughout this plateau area. They cleared the monsoonal rainforest vegetation for their fields, which were so steep, in some cases, that a farmer planting rice or corn or other cash crops had to

From an Asian Hmong house: stool, gourd water jar, and bamboo rattan table.

tether himself to a stump lest he fall off his field. The tropical highland climate meant that 40 inches of rain might fall from May through August, but upland temperatures were somewhat cooler than in the lowlands, where the Lao and Thai towns and cities were located.

Although the Hmong lived near and traded with neighboring tribal peoples such as the Mien, Akha, Lahu, and Lisu, their highly ornamented clothing set them apart. At home or working in the fields, the Hmong could be identified by their outfits combining green, pink, black, dark blue, and white, heavy with embroidery and appliqué.

Each Hmong subgroup identified themselves through different clothing. Green Hmong (sometimes

A pair of "frog legs" designs in appliqué and embroidery on a woman's burial collar.

called Blue Hmong) women wore dark blue, pleated and embroidered skirts while the White Hmong women wore unadorned white pleated skirts, or black pants for everyday. Both groups added red or pink embroidery and appliqué designs to the jacket closings, collars, aprons, sashes, leggings, and headdresses. Layers of silver jewelry appeared on special occasions. The traditional dress for Hmong men was less elaborate—loose-fitting black pants, a sash and short jacket, with embroidered panels.

The annual agriculture and sewing cycles interlocked so that a new set of clothes could be made for each person once a year. In January when men cleared the jungle by burning, women began a new round of sewing. The needles were busy as the rice and corn were planted and grew during the rainy season. The needleworkers still had to race to finish the family clothing by December when the harvest was celebrated at the New Year Festival. Hmong who wore old clothing at the festival might have bad luck during the year!

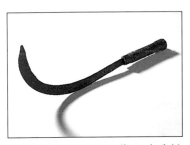

A sickle for cutting rice stalks in the field.

Some of the finest handwork commemorated births and deaths. A mother transported her baby on her back in a brilliantly decorated carrying cloth, called a *nyia* (**knee**-ah). Baby's caps were festooned with pompoms, braid, and embroidery.

Green Hmong women of Laos and Thailand also excelled in the production of *batik* fabric, used for their full pleated skirts. In the batik process, lines of melted wax are drawn on plain cloth and the cloth is dipped in wax-resistant indigo blue dye. Removal of the wax reveals an overall soft white geometric network of lines on a deep blue background. The needleworkers often embellished the batik fabric with embroidery and braid overlays in hot pink, yellow, green, and red.

Girls as young as four would watch their mothers' constant needlework and would begin the simplest designs with cotton thread, steel needle, and scraps of cloth. By the time they were 10 years old, girls knew a dozen complex cross-stitch designs and other techniques, such as satin, chain, and couching stitches, as well as appliqué, in which intricate cloth patterns are cut and sewn down in layers of contrasting colors.

Needlework artists became adept at combining symmetrical patterns and fine stitchery into "flower cloth." As their designs traced the Hmong world, they learned the significance of each motif—"snail house," "bird's wings," "lightning," "rooster combs," "frog legs," "dragon's tail," and many more.

Woman's burial sash with "snail house" in the corners and "steps" in the centers.

For 100 years the Hmong grew crops, raised pigs and chickens, stitched flower cloth tales, and lived a family-centered existence in their remote villages. But the peace was shattered in the late 1950s when the Hmong were forced to take sides in the guerrilla warfare in Laos. Some Hmong sided with the Royal Lao government backed by the United States, while other Hmong sided with the Communist Pathet Lao nationalists supported by the North Vietnamese and the Soviet Union. General Vang Pao led a Hmong army financed and trained by the American Central Intelligence Agency. In this "secret war" in Laos, thousands of Hmong men and boys were recruited by the CIA to help with rescue missions and other guerrilla operations. Hmong families

were forced to hide in the jungle as the Pathet Lao invaded their villages from the ground while the CIA bombed their villages from the air. About 40,000 Lao Hmong lost their lives in the fighting.

A baby girl's collar with curled "snail house" motifs in appliqué and embroidery.

In 1975, when the Royal Lao government fell and the United States withdrew from its northern Laos airfield command center, the Hmong allies were left in a desperate situation—some say they were abandoned to the killing fields of the Pathet Lao. Many Hmong were massacred outright in retaliation for the war. Others were interred in "camps" for "re-education" to the communist system and often they were killed or died because of the brutal conditions in the camps. An investigation by the New York-based Lawyers Committee for Human Rights concluded that between 1975 and 1980, the destruction of the Hmong reached 100,000 deaths from an estimated population of 350,000 to 400,000.

Green Hmong batik wall hanging made at the Ban Vinai refugee camp, 1988.

Thousands of displaced survivors made their way to the Mekong River (known as the Khong River to the Hmong) and hazarded the dangerous crossing by raft or floats to refuge in Thailand. Detained in refugee camps maintained by the United Nations High Commission for Refugees, the people lived minimally in multi-family, barracks-like buildings. Some were able to grow gardens. But mostly they played a waiting game to qualify for refugee emigration permits to Europe and America.

The women resumed their needlework and taught the old patterns to the girls. International relief workers began to buy flower cloth to send home. Soon Hmong refugees developed markets for the intricate needlework in France and the United States.

The people tried to live normally in the camps in Thailand. Time was heavy and many stories were told—of the "origins of the Free People," of better days in the mountain villages, and of recent trauma and flight. Hmong men and women needed to *tell,* to pass on their stories to the young people and to others. Fortunately, their strong narrative tradition and artistic needlework skill found a new means of expression well suited to the pressing need for income—the story cloth. Drawn by men and embroidered by women to document Hmong legends, lifeways, and experiences, story cloths are both family heirlooms and collectible folk art.

A pocket purse with "lightning" toward the center, in appliqué and embroidery.

"Dia's Story Cloth" is an outstanding example of this new textile art form. A double bed-sized piece of gray commercial cotton cloth is the foundation. On it, Dia's uncle, Nhia Thao Cha, drew figures and scenes of Hmong history, life, the war, and the escape. His wife Chue used chain, feather, satin, and cross stitches to render the hundreds of animals, plants, people, houses, and events. Their stories grew to fill the cloth and document the Hmong journey.

Dia's aunt and uncle even visualized the bus and the plane that carried refugees to relocation in Europe and America. The last stop for many Hmong was a city with skyscrapers and busy streets and a new, confusing life. Twenty weeks of training in language and job skills (furnished by United Nations educators) helped prepare people, and after arrival the transition was eased by private sponsors, schools, and on-the-job training. Electronics assembly companies are particularly frequent employers of Hmong still learning English. Farming—so different in the United States—is seldom an option for the refugees.

Family and clan groups are rebuilding in American communities, where too few of their neighbors recognize the extraordinary journey of the Hmong and their special relationship with the United States. They have yet to be officially honored nationally for their alliance with America during the war in Vietnam and Laos, for their bravery and their huge sacrifices as a people in the effort. And many Americans do not differentiate them from other Asian newcomers.

In common with *all* Americans, those of Hmong heritage daily face choices for change, stability, and renewal. They mix remembered ways with new lifestyles. For elders who lived in Laos and Thailand, consensus and tradition are easier to find. But the young, in their haste to develop fully

A boy's jacket, with "hearts" on the sleeves and "bird's wings" down the front.

as Americans, often have little interest in and knowledge of their roots. Just like new Americans who stood in immigration lines on Ellis Island at the turn of the 20th century, many Hmong do understand that heritage needs to be preserved both at home and in organizations, schools, and museums. As Dia Cha puts it, "We want to add something important to the rainbow of the community."

Fortunately, Hmong Americans can turn once again for identity to their unique needlework and

storytelling traditions. In their rush to escape from the war, they left behind everything. However, the women sometimes salvaged a piece or two of precious needlework. Today, in Denver or St. Paul

"Rooster combs" (or "dragon tails") in reverse appliqué and couching stitch on a contemporary sampler made for sale.

or Fresno, new heirlooms are also being created from contemporary fabrics and ornaments. Other versions are sent here by relatives in Laos, Thailand, or China. Every December the Hmong American New Year Festival is celebrated, as before, with the finest jewelry, clothing, music, and food.

With the trauma in Hmong history now giving way to a time when these Free People are faced with new freedoms in a new land, many Hmong Americans wonder whether the story cloths of coming generations will continue to tell their heritage. As Dia Cha notes, "This story cloth reminds me of the history of my family and of my people. . . . It is important to remember everything the Hmong have been through."

Americans all, can we help each other to remember and grow? The freedom to celebrate and share our cultural traditions makes life in America a rich experience. Let us *all* continue telling our stories. . . .

Hmong American woman dressed for the New Year Festival. ©DMNH

Joyce Herold
CURATOR OF ETHNOLOGY,
DENVER MUSEUM OF NATURAL HISTORY

Bibliography

Garrett, W. E. "No Place to Run: The Hmong of Laos." *National Geographic.* Vol. 157, No. 5: 78–111, Jan. 1974.

Hamilton-Merritt, Jane. *Tragic Mountains: The Hmong, the Americans, and the Secret Wars for Laos, 1942–1992.* Bloomington: Indiana University Press, 1993.

Hassel, Carla J. *Creating Pa ndau.* Lombard, IL: Wallace-Homestead Book Company, 1984.

Lewis, Paul and Elaine. *Peoples of the Golden Triangle.* London: Thames and Hudson, 1984.

Livo, Norma, and Cha, Dia. *Folk Stories of the Hmong: Peoples of Laos, Thailand and Vietnam.* Englewood, CO: Libraries Unlimited, 1991.

Peterson, Sally. "Translating Experience and the Reading of a Story Cloth." *Journal of American Folklore.* Vol. 101, No. 339: 6–22, Jan./Mar. 1988.

Quincy, Keith. *Hmong: History of a People.* Cheney, WA: Eastern Washington University Press, 1988.

Sherman, Spencer. "The Hmong in America." *National Geographic.* Vol. 174, No. 4: 586–610, Oct. 1988.

White, Virginia. *Pa Ndau: the Needlework of the Hmong.* Cheney, WA: Cheney Free Press, 1982.